Peter Blundell

BLUNDELLIAN WRITERS

1604-2004

John Hollands MC

First published 2004
Edward Gaskell *publishers*
Cranford House
6 Grenville Street
Bideford
Devon EX39 2EA

isbn 1 -898546 -70 -3

BLUNDELLIAN WRITERS

1604-2004

John Hollands MC

Printed and bound in the UK by
Lazarus Press
Unit 7 Caddsdown Business Park
Bideford
Devon
EX39 3DX
WWW.LAZARUSPRESS.COM

Lazarus Press
DEVON

CONTENTS

CONTENTS

AUTHOR'S NOTE
AND ACKNOWLEDGEMENTS

'Blundellian Writers' is part of the 400th anniversary celebrations of Blundell's School.

For the purposes of this book, 'Blundellian' is defined as someone who attended the school either as a pupil or a member of the staff. They were not necessarily members of the Old Blundellian Club. Nor have I placed any restrictions on how long they were at the school. One was there for eight years; another was expelled after a few months. . . it makes no difference.

Where possible, the House and dates of the Blundellian are included, but sometimes these are either inapplicable or unknown and therefore remain blank.

In preparing this book I have been aided by many publications, far too numerous to list. Also, many people have chipped in with help and advice. To all of them I extend my gratitude, but in particular I should mention Mrs Jenny Gordon, Blundell's Librarian, Mrs Hazel Skinner, the Tiverton Librarian, Sir John Margetson, the Blundell's Foundation, Charles Noon, Blundell's Archivist, Brian Jenkins, School Historian, Christopher Price, and Ted Crowe, Secretary of the Old Blundellian Club.

On occasions I revert to personal opinions or asides. I make no apology for this. I regard it as the author's privilege. This is not a history. It is the jottings of someone who has read about these men (and knows at least part of their works) and who is now trying to pass on the pride felt at the diversity and quality displayed by these Blundellians.

D.J. Hollands (OH 1946-1951)

INTRODUCTION

R.A. (Rab) Butler (who introduced the famous 1944 Education Act) maintained that in the long term the only true way to judge a school is by the achievements and behaviour of its ex-pupils. This does, of course, have to take into account the fact that fields of endeavour after leaving school are forever widening; and, likewise, that judgements as to what is of value to society change constantly.

However, the power, value, and importance of the written word has remained constant over the years. The pen always has been mightier than the sword, and it always will be (barring total annihilation!). So when it comes to achievements with the written word, how does Blundell's fare? What influence, enlightenment, and pleasure, has Blundell's produced in the last four hundred years?

This is a big question which this short survey cannot hope to answer. I can only sketch a vague outline of Blundellian achievements and then hope that this will whet the appetite of the reader and perhaps encourage him or her to investigate the matter further and thereby make an individual judgement.

I have mentioned the earlier Blundellian writers in approximate chronological order; but once into more modern times (around the beginning of the twentieth Century), I have split the writers into groups, according to subject matter.

With the vast expansion in technology, communications, and literacy, there are now so many writers at large that it is impossible to mention all Blundellian writers. Some have no doubt been left out due to my ignorance but others chose not to be included.

EARLY BLUNDELLIAN WRITERS

Samuel Wesley Junior (1691-1739)

It is appropriate to start with a household name, a name that has weathered the test of time. The man concerned is Samuel Wesley the younger, being the eldest son of Samuel Wesley and brother of John Wesley, founder of Methodism. He was the eleventh headmaster of Blundell's (this includes the first one who lasted less than a day!). He accepted the position in 1733 and retained it until his death in 1739.

Before taking up this position he had already been ordained and had a formidable reputation as a man of letters, being well-known in London for his satire and humorous verses. In 1736 he produced a volume of verse entitled 'Poems on Several Occasions', the success of which can be judged by it going into several editions.

Earlier, he had produced several other notable works: in 1716 'Neck or Nothing'; in 1724 'The Song of the Three Children' and 'The Battle of the Sexes'; in 1732 'The Parish Priest'; and in 1735 'The Christian Poet'.

Like his brother John, Samuel Wesley Junior was chronically nearsighted. He also suffered from general ill health and he died suddenly, but not unexpectedly, in Tiverton on Nov 6th 1739.

Stephen Weston (1747—1830)

Stephen Weston was one of Blundell's most prolific writers. He went to Blundell's in 1760 before passing on to Exeter College, Oxford.

Most of his literary output came after his wife died towards the end of the 18th Century. He then moved to London and became a notable figure among the literary elite, including many lady admirers. He is said to have had around fifty books published, consisting mainly of oriental translations, descriptions of travel, theological treatises, and books on one of his great passions in life: Paris.

Indeed, he was in the French capital at the time of the Revolution and only fled back to England during the latter stages, many said experiencing a narrow escape.

He was a regular contributor to the *Gentleman's Magazine*, *Literary Anecdotes*, and the *Classics Journal*. Many of his poems were signed 'W.N.' His portrait, probably by Joshua Reynolds, hangs in hall at Exeter College, Oxford.

John Rendle (1758-1815)

When John Rendle attended Blundell's he was already a noted classics scholar. He then went on to Sidney Sussex College, Cambridge. He became a fellow of the College and lecturer in mathematics. He spent most of his life at Widecombe, where he died. His writing concentrated on early Christian history and he had an enormously high reputation among the intellectuals of his day. Perhaps his major work was 'The History of Tiberius', a learned work vindicating the character of the emperor, claiming that he was a convert to Christianity, and a great patron of it. Rendle was also author of several important papers on biblical criticism in the *Orthodox Churchman's Magazine*.

William Buckland (1784-1856)

William Buckland was born in Axminster, the son of the rector of Templeton and Trusham. He was one of the most remarkable individuals Blundell's has ever produced. He attended the school in the late 1790s and he was noted for his extraordinary powers of observation and offbeat interests, principal among which were sponges and other fossils. From Blundell's he went up to Corpus Christi College, Oxford, where he further developed his interest in fossils and geology generally. In 1813 Buckland was appointed to the chair of mineralogy at Oxford and in the same year became a fellow of the Geological Society of London.

Buckland was elected a fellow of the Royal Society in 1818 and throughout this period was producing papers and lectures in abundance. The lectures were highly acclaimed because of his brilliant and humorous delivery. In 1825 he married and made no secret of the fact that his wife was of great value to him in producing his most famous work, the Bridgwater Treatise. This appeared in 1836 and aimed to illustrate the power, wisdom, and goodness of God in his creation.

In 1845, Buckland became Dean of Westminster which is said to have made him abandon many of his former pursuits.

However, according to the Catalogue of Scientific Papers published by the Royal Society, Buckland was the author of fifty-three major works. In 1840 he was elected President of the Geological Society for the second time. Shortly afterwards he was struck down by a mental disease which prevented him from carrying out any further work. When he died in 1856 he was widely mourned by all those who had listened to his eloquence or who had been charmed by the strange truths which he had discovered from his study of nature.

William Harding (1792-1886)

William Harding only published one book. However, this became accepted as the definitive history of Tiverton. . . . greatly admired in all quarters.

He was a pupil at Blundell's in the early 1800s and then became an ensign in the North Devon Militia. Most of his service was with Wellington in the Peninsular wars, including the siege of Burgos, the capture of Madrid, and the battles of Vittoria, Nivelle, Nive, and Toulouse. He retired as a Lieutenant Colonel and then devoted himself to the history of Tiverton.

It is worth noting that there have been four recognised histories of Tiverton, all by Old Blundellians. First was John Blundell's 'Memoirs' in 1712; then Martin Dunsford's 'Historical Memoirs of the Town and Parish' in 1792; thirdly Harding's book in two volumes; and finally one by FJ Snell, who is mentioned later. A fifth history of Tiverton is due to be published shortly, not written by a Blundellian, but with a strong Blundellian influence.

Abraham Hayward (1801-1884)

Hayward was an essayist who liked to regard himself as a self-made man, mainly because when he first went to London as an adult he was lonesome and led a solitary life. He was educated at Blundell's from 1811 to 1817 and did not take to the school on account of its harsh discipline and poor food.

However, it is recorded that he learnt how to swim and fish, apparently his only accomplishments in an otherwise undistinguished school career. On leaving school he was articled to a solicitor in Ilchester, but this was also not to his liking and he soon became a student at the Inner Temple.

In 1828 the first number of the *Law Magazine* appeared under the joint editorship of W. Cornish and A. Hayward. It soon established a fine reputation and before long Hayward was in sole charge as editor, a position he retained until 1844. In 1833 he published a translation of 'Faust' with splendid reviews. This set him up in London society and from then onwards his talents as a reviewer were in constant demand and he also went on to write on a wide range of subjects, such as 'Some Account of a Journey Across the Alps'; 'Verses of Other Days'; 'The Art of Dining'; and many more.

Thomas Hayter (1702-1762)

Hayter was successively Bishop of Norwich and London. He was essentially a Devonian and his family has a long connection with Chagford, on Dartmoor. This has lasted until the present day in the form of the Hayter-Hames family.

Thomas Hayter was educated at Blundell's during the 1715-20 period and then followed the path so many Blundellians have trod by going up to Balliol College, Oxford. He later went on to Emmanuel College, Cambridge for his MA degree and DD.

His career was very controversial and his success was due to good contacts and influence in high places. He became private chaplain to Archbishop Lancelot Blackbume of York. There was even gossip that Hayter was Blackbume's natural son, but this was never firmly established. He was also involved in the education of the Prince of Wales but this did not go smoothly and eventually resulted in his resignation.

Hayter was author of several highly influential works, principal among which were, 'An Account of the Prosecutions of the People Called Quakers', and 'An Essay on the Liberty of the Press'. Many of his more notable sermons were also committed to print.

Richard Hoblyn (1803-1886)

Richard Hoblyn was principally a writer on education and science. He was born in Colchester but was educated at Blundell's around 1816-20. His connection with the school, and his reason for being sent there, are unknown. After Blundell's he went to Balliol College, Oxford, and then into the Church; but he soon resigned in order to concentrate on teaching and writing on educational topics. During this period he was based in the Marylebone region of London.

His principal works were: "A Dictionary of Terms Used in Medicine and the Collateral Sciences'; 'A Manual of Chemistry'; 'A Manual of the Steam Engine'; A Manual of Natural Philosophy'; and 'A Dictionary of Scientific Terms'.

Alexander Knox (1818-1891)

Knox went to Blundell's in the early 1830s and then progressed to Trinity College, Cambridge. He was never a very robust person and spent much of his time in southern climes, on one occasion travelling with Shelley's widow and her son Percy, a friend of his from Cambridge days.

In 1844 he was called to the Bar as a member of Lincoln's Inn and in 1846 he started writing leading articles as a staff member of *The Times*. He continued in this capacity until 1860. Knox enjoyed a high reputation as a linguist and a brilliant conversationalist. Principal among his books were 'The New Playground, Or Wandering in Algeria', 1881. He was also a regular contributor to the *Edinburgh Review*, *Blackwood*, and many other periodicals.

Charles Chesney (1826-1876)

Chesney was born into a military family, the nephew of General Rawden Chesney. His early education was left to his gifted mother, but she eventually sent him to Blundell's where he distinguished himself in many respects. In 1843 he went to the Royal Military Academy at Woolwich, being commissioned in 1845.

A posting to New Zealand was cut short by ill health but he then got the post of Professor of Military History at the Cadet School, Woolwich, and then at the Staff College at Sandhurst. At the latter, he soon became recognised as the foremost military critic of his day, especially noted for the way he made his students take a more scientific view of their profession. His lectures were not only clear and logical, but in their own way revolutionary. It was a daring step to subject the American Civil War to military criticism whilst it was still in progress.

'Campaigns in Virginia and Maryland' was published in 1863 and his 'Waterloo' lectures were published in 1868. These were not only adopted as textbook instructions in the British army, but also in France and Germany, the main feature of the lectures being complete impartiality. Other works included, 'The Tactical Use of Fortresses'; 'The Military Resources of Prussia and France'; and 'Essays in Military Biography'. He was also a frequent contributor to the *Edinburgh Review* and *Fraser's Magazine*.

Tragically, whilst serving as a Lt-Colonel at Aldershot, he caught a chill which led to his death at the age of forty-nine.

Samuel Reynolds (1831-1897)

In February 1847, Samuel Reynolds went to Blundell's, but he stayed there a comparatively short time, going instead to Radley as one of its original pupils. He later wrote a book (1897) about his experiences at this new school. He then went on to Exeter College, Oxford, where he won the Newdigate poetry prize and then the Chancellor's prize for English, on account of his essay on 'The Reciprocal Action of the Physical and Moral Condition of Countries upon each Other'. He became an MA in 1857 and although for some years he remained in university life, he joined the staff of *The Times* and from 1873 until 1896 he contributed regularly, producing over 2,000 articles on a variety of topics, from literature to politics and finance. These were later brought out in volume form after his death as 'Studies of Many Subjects'. He was regarded by his contemporaries as a man of engaging social qualities, being an excellent raconteur with a very caustic wit. His literary style was said to be lucid and terse.

Sir George Chesney (1830-1895)

Sir George was a brother of Charles Chesney and was also a military man. He was born in Tiverton and educated at Blundell's, where his early thoughts turned towards a medical career. This was soon abandoned when he was awarded an Indian cadetship and attended the Military College of the East India Company at Addiscombe. Then followed a military career in various parts of India, during which he was decorated for bravery during the Indian Mutiny.

His interest centred on engineering and his first published work was a discourse on the financing of public works. Then followed a work, 'A View of the System of Administration in India'. In 1871, while President of the Royal Indian Civil Service Engineering College at Staines, he contributed a brilliant article to Blackwood's Magazine entitled, 'The Battle of Dorking'. This enjoyed enormous popularity, being based on an imaginary invasion of England by a foreign power. This proved so popular that it was brought out as a book and was reprinted many times. Then followed a full scale novel, 'The True Reformer', the keynote of which was army reform. His next novel was entitled, 'The Dilemma' which dealt with the character of Indian troops.

After another distinguished spell in India where he worked alongside Lord Roberts, he returned to England and was elected as a Conservative member for Oxford. He died suddenly and was buried at Englefield Green. His other novels included 'The New Ordeal'; 'The Private Secretary'; and 'The Lesters, or a Capitalist's Labour'.

George Body (1840-1911)

George Body was another Blundellian who was devoted to a religious life. He attended Blundell's from 1849 to 1857 (one wonders what he did during all that time) and then tried to establish himself as a missionary. However, ill health forced him to change his plans and he went up to St John's College, Cambridge, becoming MA in 1876. He was then ordained and eventually progressed through Wolverhampton and the Black Country to become Canon of Durham where he gained a splendid reputation for his work among the coal miners.

His published works were mainly devotional, but he clearly had a good eye for catchy titles, including 'The Life of Justification'; 'The Life of Temptation'; 'The Present State of the Departed'; 'The Appearance of the Risen Lord'; and the 'The Work of Grace in Paradise'.

R.D. Blackmore (1825-1900)

Richard Doddridge Blackmore is unchallenged as the finest writer Blundell's School has produced in its 400 years. As is often the case, his fame (and fortune) came from one title, 'Lorna Doone'. Ironically, it was by no means Blackmore's favourite among his many novels. He placed it third in order of merit after 'Maid of Sker' and 'Springhaven'.

*RD
Blackmore*

A point which is often missed about Blackmore (and which he probably missed himself being so close to the subject) was that he, more than anyone else, popularised a whole new trend in English literature. He took readers away from the socially aware novels of Dickens and Thackeray and established the new romantic movement which relied on melding romance with historical fact and authentic backgrounds. Indeed, with his gift for descriptive writing, the settings of his novels never failed to strike home to his readers and make them feel as though they were actually there. It was claimed for him that he did for Devon what Scott did for the Highlands.

Another thing Blackmore achieved, where so many other famous authors failed, was to create heroines who acted and thought like real people, far from the cardboard cut-out which readers were so accustomed to. In particular, Amy Rosedew and Lorna Doone must surely go down as two of literature's most fascinating and believable heroines.

Blackmore had a curious career at Blundell's. He claimed to have been bullied and as a junior he was certainly no admirer of the fagging system. He was reported to be a shy, quick-witted, and humorous boy with a touch of mischief ever present. A close friend of his at Blundell's was Frederick Temple (later the Archbishop). At one time, whilst living at Culmstock, Temple took lessons from Blackmore's father, who was a noted scholar of his day.

Despite reports of Blackmore's early unhappiness at Blundell's, he nevertheless rose to be Head Boy. As such he no doubt took full advantage of the fagging system, this time without complaint. From Blundell's he went to his father's old college at Oxford (Exeter) and gained a MA in 1852, the same year as he was also called to the Bar. For a short time he stuck with the law but he soon decided to concentrate on writing, his real love being poetry. His first published book was 'Poems by Melanter' which – in modern parlance – sank without trace. Other books of poems followed and also a translation of Theocritus which appeared in *Fraser's Magazine*.

It wasn't until he moved to the tranquillity of a lovely house and garden in Twickenham that Blackmore, somewhat disillusioned by his lack of success with poetry, turned to writing novels. His first, 'Clara Vaughan', appeared in 1864 and had a luke-warm reception. Then, in 1869, his third novel, 'Lorna Doone', established him as a great novelist.

Twelve more novels followed 'Lorna Doone' and all of them were characterised by a link with Blackmore's own life and character. After he had turned seventy, he returned to his first love, poetry, and one of the penalties he suffered as a result of the enormous success of 'Lorna Doone' was that his poetry was underrated. Anyone who has read his poem 'Dominus Illuminatio Mea' will surely realise that as a writer R.D. Blackmore was a genius. He stands among the truly great in English literature.

Archbishop Temple

E. Hutton (1875-1969)

Apart from living to a ripe old age, Hutton was best known for his deep interest and love of Italy. After his schooling at Blundell's he chose to go there as a tutor rather than take a place at Oxford University. He served with the Foreign Office, but retained his contacts with Italy. He became a Cavaliere of the Crown of Italy and when he was aged 83 Italy conferred on him one of their highest honours, the Commenda of the Ordine Per Il Perto Della Republica. As though this were not enough, when he turned 90 he was presented with Italy's highest Cultural Award.

Hutton published 'Florence' in 1952 and then many other books on Italy. He also published 'Highways and Byways of Somerset', and other volumes on Wiltshire and Gloucestershire.

Frederick Temple (1821-1902)

To end the section on early Blundellian writers with Frederick Temple is fitting: although he cannot compare with his friend and contemporary Richard Blackmore as a man of letters he is – without much serious argument – the most distinguished of all Old Blundellians, his fame coming not so much from being Archbishop of Canterbury, but his achievements when he occupied that august position in the years 1897 to 1902.

Temple was of good birth, related to the Duke of Buckingham on his father's side and the Earl of Warwick on his mother's side. He was the thirteenth and youngest survivor of fifteen children and on the death of his father he found himself living in Culmstock. For a time he was educated by his gifted mother, but then went to Blundell's in May 1834. He remained at the school until 1839, during which time he gave ample proof of his ability and industry. In six months he passed through the Lower School to the Upper School, something which usually required at least two years.

From Blundell's he went up to Balliol and, although in precarious financial straits, made the most of the opportunities offered by Balliol. One of his tutors, Tait, later became Archbishop of Canterbury and there is no doubt that he was a great influence throughout Temple's career. It was due to his helping hand that Temple became headmaster of Rugby School in 1857.

It was during his headmastership that he became involved with the notorious publication 'Essays and Reviews' (1865). In today's climate, with religious principles and doctrines being thrown overboard on a regular basis, it is diffiult for us to realise what an enormous storm of protest these Essays caused. Temple's contribution was 'Education of the World', which in terms of controversy was innocuous enough. His real crime was one of associating with disruptive elements such as Rowland Williams (who denied the inspiration of the scriptures), and Henry Wilson (who denied the doctrine of eternal punishment).

By associating with such rogues, and by refusing to retract, Temple nearly lost the chance to become Bishop of Exeter. However, once he had been consecrated in 1869 he withdrew his essay from the later editions of 'Essays and Reviews'.

Temple was enthroned in Canterbury as Archbishop in 1897 and became one of the most active and influential Arhbishops ever known, expressing his decidedly liberal views on many occasions in the House of Lords.

Temple's chief published works were: 'Sermons Preached at Rugby'; 'Quiet Growth' (a sermon delivered at Clifton College); 'The Three Spiritual Revelations'; 'Relationship between Religion and Science'; and 'Five of the Latest Utterances of Frederick Temple'.

The Archbishop died at Lambeth Palace on December 22nd 1902 and was buried in the cloister of Canterbury Cathedral.

MODERN WRITERS

Novelists, Poets, and Literature

It is often claimed (particularly by novelists) that the novel is the highest form of art. If this is so, it is something which Old Blundellians need to gloss over fairly smartly. Looking back over 400 years of the school's history, there is an inexplicable dearth of top novelists. Sir George Chesney had considerable success, as we have already seen; and the achievements of R.D. Blackmore would keep most schools happy for several generations. However, in more recent times, in which the novel has expanded at an enormous rate, Blundell's has a poor track record in keeping pace.

Only one Old Blundellian* since Blackmore has become a truly international, best-selling, novelist. What makes this all the more surprising is that **DJ Hollands (OH 1946-51)** started his Blundell's career at the bottom of 4a and spent more time in 5x (failed exams, try again) than anyone before or since. However, his antiwar novel, 'The Dead, the Dying and the Damned', based on the Korean war (in which he served as a National Service subaltern), has been published throughout the world and notched up sales in excess of 3 million copies. It was also acclaimed by the world's press and on numerous occasions linked with 'All Quiet on the Western Front' as the finest portrayal of infantrymen at war.

At one time in the United States (before the advent of the

*This section has been contributed
by L.M.C. Pyne .

John Hollands

'internet') 'The Dead, the Dying and the Damned' was a cult book changing hands at anything up to $260 a copy.

The book was originally inspired by Hollands' English teacher, Peter Brooke-Smith, who told him that his only chance of success as a novelist was to volunteer for Korea so that he at least had something worthwhile to write about. Since then, Hollands has written a further eight novels, but none of them has achieved the same success as 'The Dead, the Dying and the Damned'. Two of them, 'Not Shame the Day' and 'The Exposed' were also based in the Far East, but Hollands has now embarked on his most ambitious project yet: 'Memory and Imagination', the Memoirs of an Anglo-Indian which will run into at least four volumes.

A contemporary of Hollands in Old House was **Robin Lloyd-Jones (OH 1949-52)** and he too has enjoyed success as a novelist. He has twice been nominated for the Booker Prize and in his first attempt he reached the 'long-list' (last twenty). His novels have attracted several awards and all of them have been hailed by critics in the national press. The two novels nominated for the Booker Prize were: 'Lord of the Dance' and

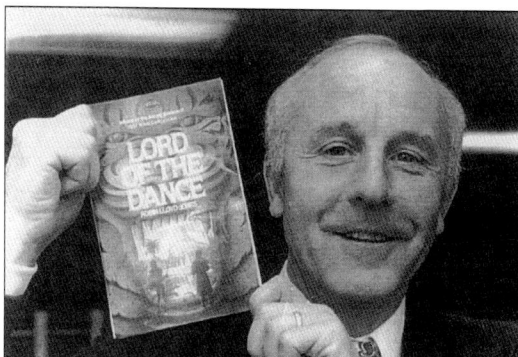

Robin
Lloyd-Jones

'The Dream House'. 'Lord of the Dance' was also published in the States and Spain. It won the BBC Bookshelf First Novel Award.

Lloyd-Jones has likewise had success in broadcasting. His drama 'Ice In Wonderland' won the BBC Best Radio Drama Script Award in 1994. When Lloyd-Jones ended his days at Blundell's he went up to Cambridge and then became a teacher, finally becoming a Director of a Curriculum Development Centre, followed by an Adviser in Education. He took early retirement in 1989 in order to concentrate on his writing. At the moment he is busy writing two books, 'Shadows on the Lawn', an account of growing up in India during the last years of the Raj, and 'Trickster Amazed' a novel set in the 14th century.

Since 1991 Lloyd-Jones has been tutor in Creative Writing at Glasgow University and has also served as President of the Scottish branch of PEN International.

The most consistent and prolific of Blundellian novelists in recent years is **Michael Gilbert (SH 1926-31)**. He has now retired, but in his day he churned out books at the rate of two or three a year and had numerous honours bestowed upon him. Yet he never achieved the big breakthrough with a major best seller. His main interest was in crime novels, but he also

Molesworth

wrote short stories and radio plays. He was a founder member of the Crime Writers' Association and he was given the Swedish Grand Master Award in 1981. He also had a big following in America and was presented with the Edgar Allan Poe Grand Master Award of the Mystery Writers of America in 1987. Gilbert also had a distinguished career in other areas. He gained a law degree at London University and was a senior member in a Lincoln's Inn partnership. In the Second World War he served in North Africa and Italy. In 1989 the *New Yorker* wrote of him: 'Michael Gilbert is one of the few remaining masters of the classic English murder mystery'.

Geoffrey Willans (Petergate) was more of a humorist than a novelist, specialising in short books about the adventures of a delightful prep-school boy named Molesworth. The books, of which there were several, had a large following in the late fifties and early sixties and were notable for the illustrations of Ronald Searle of St. Trinian's fame.

Whilst such Blundellian successes are few and far between in the field of novels, one should not be despondent about the future. Not only are Lloyd-Jones and Hollands still writing (and convinced that their best work is yet to come), but great hopes are pinned on **Ben Rice (TH 1986-91)**. Rice is the son of a former Blundell's master and as well as accumulating prizes for his poetry whilst still at school, he was recently nominated by *Granta* Magazine as one of Britain's most promising young writers. So far, he has only published a novella, 'Pobby and Dingan', but this became a BBC 'Book at Bedtime' and it has been published in many different languages, to say nothing of carrying high hopes for a feature film. In short, Ben Rice is a name to watch out for.

When it comes to poetry, the field opens up considerably. What is little known is that one of the finest of the First World War Poets was a Blundellian, **Arthur Grahame West**. Whilst all the accolades usually go to Owen and Sassoon, the fact is that West's poetry related far more to the attitude of Tommy Atkins, without the personal bitterness of the disillusioned

*Sir John Squire
with poet
Edmund Blunden*

intellectuals. West did not enjoy good health at Blundell's and this frailty and love of books did not lead to happy school-days. Certainly, he should never have been sent anywhere near the Flanders trenches. However, he insisted on volunteering and he was duly killed in the long term interests of us all. His major poems appeared after he died, as did his successful book, ironically entitled, 'Diary of a Dead Officer'.

A notable thing about the First World War poetry was an absence of humour. This was redressed to a degree by **Sir John Squire (SH 1901–1903)**. In his book of verse protesting against the war, 'The Survival of the Fittest', he had the lines:

God heard the embattled nations sing and shout
Gott straffe England and God save the king,
God this, God that, and God the other thing,
Good God, said God, I've got my work cut out.

As befitting someone who was born on April Fool's Day 1884, Sir John Squire became one of England's most memorable eccentrics, yet an eccentric who still managed to reach the peak of his profession as a poet, literary critic, and editor of the literary magazine *London Mercury*. Sir John was not the world's greatest poet, nor was he the world's greatest editor, but he most certainly was the world's worst cricketer. That is no insult, for there are legions of flannelled fools who would give their right arm for that title; but against Sir John they stood no chance. If one reads the village cricket match scene in 'England Their England' by A.G. Macdonell, one soon finds out why. If one accepts that there is more to cricket than Test Matches, one has also to acknowledge that no man has ever influenced our noble national game in a more delightful way. Sir John was a prolific writer and could be a caustic critic. He championed lyrical poetry and once, when reviewing T.S. Eliot's 'The Waste Land', he wrote in the *London Mercury*:

'I've read it several times and am still unable to make head or tail of it. Will someone please take me to a pub?'

As he grew older he experienced hard times financially. He also became completely bizarre in his dress. He once visited the Athenaeum in white flannels, black evening slippers, a moth-eaten polo-neck pullover, a shirt with a winged collar, and an Old Blundellian tie.

He died peacefully at 74. The importance of his career can be summed up by what happened at the Dorchester Hotel in 1932. A full house of 500 literary personalties gathered to celebrate his achievements. The first speaker was G.K. Chesterton who said, 'As editor of the *London Mercury* Jack Squire will remain for centuries as an example of a man who controlled creative power'.

Among the Blundellian poets, one who will need little introduction is **Stephen Spender**. He came to Blundell's to teach English during the second world war. Although of an age for the armed forces, he was a volunteer fireman and was

Mark Aldridge

Stephen Spender

persuaded to teach at Blundell's by his great friend Cecil Day Lewis, who was teaching at a lesser known school in Dorset. Spender didn't stay long at Blundell's and it is doubtful if he ever wrote much poetry while there, being the conscientious type of person who devoted all his energy to teaching.

According to **Mark Aldridge (OH 1936-1941)** – another Blundellian writer who was a pupil at the time – Cecil Day Lewis would sometimes visit Blundell's and there would be general jollifications, with Spender's beautiful fiancée, Natasha Litvin, performing on the piano. She was a fine concert pianist who later played several times at the Proms. Aldridge also tells us that Spender was an extremely good teacher, but the same could not, unfortunately, be said about another famous Blundellian writer who taught at the school at that time: **Professor C. Northcote Parkinson**.

Whether any of Parkinson's Laws (for which he soon became world famous) were inspired by Blundell's is unknown. Aldridge obviously doubts it since he describes him as bone idle and totally disinterested in teaching anything. He was first and foremost a naval historian and he could not wait to take up an appointment at B.R.N.C. Dartmouth. As Aldridge puts it, 'At Blundell's, he marked time, not his pupils' work.' Aldridge recounts that Professor Parkinson also issued a list of essay titles from which his pupils could take their pick. These do at least reveal Parkinson's sense of humour. A few samples are:

'Can you do anything with bayonets except sit on them?'
'London is a riddle: Paris is the answer.'
'Only countries where grand opera flourishes have produced fascism.'

As you can gather, Mark Aldridge's booklet, 'The Happiest Days. . .' is a marvellously evocative account of war-time Blundell's. Later in life, when he retired as a Prep School headmaster, he produced other, more intellectual, works, very often translations of poetry.

Another Old Blundellian who made an impact on literature was **Gilbert Phelps (Master 1943-45)** who taught English in the mid-forties. His is a curious tale. He could well have settled into Blundell's for the duration but he was so dismayed by the antics of the headmaster (R.L. Roberts) that he not only left Blundell's (together with several other notable teachers) but branched out into an entirely new career. First he went into broadcasting and later became an examiner for the Oxford and Cambridge Board. Finally, he concentrated on writing. In 1978 he became a Fellow of the Royal Society of Literature and as well as writing several novels, he specialised in the history of literature. His best-known and major work, which came out in a splendid Folio Society edition, was 'A Short History of English Literature'. He died in 1993.

Godfrey Bullard (SH 1943-1948) was a young poet of great promise whilst at Blundell's. In 1946 he won the Keats Prize as well as the Latin Prose Prize in 1947 and 1948. He was also a leading member of Sam Burton's Literary Society. From Blundell's he went up to Oxford and then became a school master, having picked up several more awards for his poetry along the way.

However, it wasn't until he retired in 1992 that he again took up poetry in a serious way in response to the weekly competitions in the *Spectator*. In eight years, from 1996 to 2004, he has had over fifty pieces printed by that Magazine. Another periodical to use his work regularly was the *Oxford Magazine* and he also came second in a nation-wide poetry competition organised by Radio Four.

Laurence Sail (Master 1975-1981) is another who has had considerable success with poetry. His 'World Returning' was recently published by Bloodaxe Books and was well received by the critics. Previous to that he has had published, 'Out of Land: New and Selected Poems' (1992) and 'Building into Air'.

Clem Thomas

SPORTS WRITERS

Blundell's has never had any difficulty in producing top class sportsmen, whether at cricket and rugby, or lesser known sports such as track running and shooting. The School even produced a member of the Canadian Olympic Bobsleigh team. Some of these sportsmen have written at length about their sport, usually as journalists. Those who have gone a step further and had books published have actually written them themselves – a pretty rare occurrence in sport.

Clem Thomas (FH 1943-1947) hailed from the Swansea area. As a schoolboy he was so outstanding at rugby that everyone forecast high honours for him. His progress in the game was also enhanced by the fact that, although he was one of the healthiest and most robust persons imaginable, he failed his army medical, thus enabling him to go to Cambridge and get on with the serious business of Rugby Union. His playing achievements are a matter of record: Cambridge, Swansea, Wales, and the British Lions. His most notable contribution to rugby literature was his book 'The History of the British Lions'. This is the definitive book about the Lions and the feature of it is that whilst being absolutely fair in all his comments, he never pulls any punches. He deplores the fact that rugby is no longer a game, but war, and he singles out the disgraceful treatment dished out to his fellow Old Blundellian, Richard Sharp, whilst playing for the Lions in South Africa.

For many years Clem Thomas was the rugby critic for the *Observer* and many would claim that he was among the top rugby journalists the game has known. He appeared almost as regularly on television, usually featuring with 'expert' summaries and comments. Those who watched him never failed to note that he was about the only 'expert' who was willing to make firm predictions: not for Clem any humming and hawing and sitting on the fence. He wasn't always right, of course, but he knew his mind and he expressed his opinions with dazzling clarity in a rich, English accent.

Clem was also a fine cricketer as a schoolboy: a fast bowler of the 'brute strength and ignorance' variety. He once polished off a lesser known school in Dorset almost single handed.

Usually sitting near Clem in the press boxes of all our major rugby grounds would be **Richard Sharp (W 1952-1957)**. He was in stark contrast to Clem: a lean fly half instead of a robust wing forward, an attacker rather than a defender. Whereas Clem captained Wales, Richard captained England. It was once said of Sharp that to watch him run was like watching Nureyev jump, and they should certainly have teamed up together, but at rugby not ballet: Richard would not have been a pretty sight in tights.

After his playing days, Sharp soon gained a vast and loyal following for his rugby reports for the *Sunday Telegraph*. When reading them, one soon came to appreciate that he had an enormously deep knowledge of the game, even though when watching him play he seemed to do everything by instinct.

In 1968 Sharp wrote a successful book entitled 'Winning Rugby'. This included a very interesting and honest account of his playing days at Blundell's under the coaching of

*Richard
Sharp*

Grahame Parker, Ted Crowe, and C.H.P. Silk. It has always been a disappointment to the writer of these notes that Richard Sharp has not written further books on rugby. However, there is still plenty of time.

Victor Marks (FH 1968-73) was one of those curious cricketers who started as a star batsman and useful bowler and ended up playing for England as a star bowler and useful batsman. Denis Compton did the same thing, only the other way round. Vic turned out to be just as good an all-rounder when his playing days were over and he turned to journalism. He has not only written several books on cricket but he has also become a regular member of the famous B.B.C. Test Match Special team. When he joined the *Observer* as their cricket correspondent he shared a desk with Clem Thomas; shared in the sense that Clem used it in the winter and Vic in the summer. Whether writing about cricket or talking about it

Vic Marks, bowling

in the commentary box, all Vic Marks's efforts are characterised by a lively sense of humour, a virtue that always has relevance and is linked to the game.

Grahame Parker (Master 1946-68) was probably Blundell's greatest sportsman. This view is based on his all-round ability at the very highest level in two of our major sports. He played rugby as fullback for England shortly before the war and gained a tremendous reputation as a kicker of the ball: up to that point he was probably the finest kicker the game had ever known, as he demonstrated against Ireland in 1937 when he scored 15 points with his boot. He also captained Cambridge at cricket and went on to play regularly for Gloucestershire in the golden days of Wally Hammond and Charlie Barnett. He later became captain of Devon and then secretary and president of Gloucestershire C.C.; and on his retirement he wrote a history of the club which was welcomed as a worthy addition to cricket literature. He then started on a biography of W.G. Grace but found the 'Grand Old Man of Cricket' to have been such an unsavoury character that he ditched it. Those who knew Grahame would consider such a gesture as typical, and in a very strange way his contempt for those who deserved it was one of his more endearing qualities. As a coach of rugby three-quarters he was quite outstanding and, with Ted Crowe (the author of '100 Years of Blundell's Rugby') looking after the forwards, they produced many fine sides and several international players, men like Clem Thomas, Richard Sharp, Sean McDermott, and David Shepherd.

Grahame Parker was also Blundell's cricket coach for many years, but in this regard he never reached the same heights. When boys got clean bowled he was inclined to say, "Well, there it is!" and leave it at that.

Another cricketer who has broken into print is **Hugh Morris (W 1976-82)**. His achievements as a Test Match Cricketer for England (despite being Welsh) are relatively recent, with caps against the West Indies and Sri Lanka in the early 1990s. However, he will probably be best remembered for his inspirational leadership of Glamorgan. In 2001 he produced a book 'To Lord's with a Title' which covers Glamorgan's first County Championship title in 28 years. In this book Hugh gives a fascinating insight into the workings, stresses, and strains, of first class cricket. He is also strong on giving vivid pen-portraits of some of the leading cricket personalities he played with. Now retired from playing, he has remained in the game on the coaching side. Indeed, as Technical Director of the England and Wales Cricket Board he is one of the most influential men in the game. Hopefully, more cricket books will follow from his pen.

Getting away from the more conventional sports, an Old Blundellian by the name of **Norman Clark (1907-1911)** wrote a very entertaining book about boxing which was published in 1935: 'All in the Game'. A boxer by nature, Clark was quite capable of looking after himself in the physical environment of Blundell's in those days, and he clearly enjoyed his four years at the school. One of his greatest joys was going to Aldershot where the military ran a Public Schools Boxing Championship. Clark was never a champion, but was narrowly beaten on points by the boy reckoned to be the most outstanding schoolboy boxer of the era.

Clark became a top man in British boxing. At one time he was secretary of the British Boxing Board of Control and also a very highly rated judge at the National Sporting Club. His book is an entertaining and informative collection of reminiscences and opinions.

In his book, Clark also branches out into cricket which was his second love, especially Somerset. Flying, yachting, and even roller skating also feature. In addition there are chapters on sailing around the coast of Devon and Cornwall, with a touch of travel in the West Indies thrown in. One of our most colourful Old Blundellians.

These notes on sports writing must conclude on a rather curious note. We come to the only female, **Eileen Hollands,** mentioned in this survey; but Eileen was neither a Blundellian Mistress nor one of the first girls to pioneer Blundell's co-education as a sixth-former. Strictly speaking she wasn't a Blundellian at all. In fact, in a sense, she wasn't even female. She was the pen name of the Hollands already mentioned under novelists, he of the Korean War. Writing as 'Eileen' (for obvious reasons, since in those days he could not claim to be married to a bloke) John Hollands wrote two books on sport: 'Never Marry a Cricketer' and 'Never Marry a Rugby Player'. It was to have a been a humorous series covering most sports from a woman's perspective, but when 'Never Marry a Rugby Player' came out, the real Eileen read the books and promptly brought everything to a premature and messy end by filing for divorce, something the thoroughly incompetent Judge granted with indecent alacrity.

JOURNALISTS

These days journalism covers a multitude of activities. For the purposes of this book, only journalists of the old-fashioned, conventional, type are mentioned.

Heading the list of Blundellian journalists is **Sir Gordon Newton (P 1921-26)**. To most people his name will be unfamiliar but he was one of the most important editors of his generation. He was editor of *The Financial Times* from 1949 to 1972 and during that time he established it as the most influential paper in the land; worldwide, second only to the *Wall Street Journal*. Whilst papers like *The Times* and the *Daily Express* lost their way, and their enormous influence, *The Financial Times* went from strength to strength, relying on the basic journalistic principle of giving its readers what they wanted and needed. During Sir Gordon's editorship he introduced many new features, changed the layout, and subtantially increased the circulation. Above all, he stuck to the conviction that *The Financial Times* must remain essentially financial, not a general newspaper. The paper today still has Sir Gordon's stamp all over it.

As a boy at Blundell's, Newton found life pretty tough to start with, especially since his House Master, the Reverend

Sir Gordon Newton

Granlund, did nothing to intervene even when there were near riot conditions. However, Newton had the advantage of being a fine athlete and once he had surprised everyone by matriculating with distinctions, he thoroughly enoyed his remaining three years at the school. His sporting record at Blundell's must be hard to beat: having already won the junior Russell, he became a member of the cricket and rugby 1st teams, was captain of athletics, and won the mile, the half mile, and the quarter mile events.

From Blundell's he went up to Sidney Sussex, Cambridge, and then – after war service in the Royal Artillery – into journalism. He was knighted in 1966 and then enjoyed a long retirement, eventually dying aged 90 at his home at Henley-on-Thames. His memoirs, 'A Peer Without Equal' were published in 1997, edited by Malcolm Rutherford.

Vernon Bartlett (P 1906-1910) was of slightly earlier vintage than Sir Gordon Newton but it would seem that he had a similar view of Blundell's and Petergate. However, he contrasted to Newton as a journalist, being much more the 'go-getter' news-hound as opposed to a desk-bound editor. Indeed, Vernon Bartlett found success in practically every form of writing, and was also a highly accomplished broadcaster.

Vernon Bartlett left Blundell's in time to serve in the Flanders trenches where he was twice badly wounded, an experience which made him determined to try to prevent any further world wars.

He became a reporter on the *Daily Mail* and later joined Reuters to cover the Paris Peace Conference. Then he went on to *The Times,* covering sensitive cities such as Geneva, Berlin, Rome, and Warsaw. In 1922 he became the London director of the League of Nations until 1932. Then followed a curious incident when he supported Nazi Germany's walk-out from a disarmament conference and their subsequent resignation from the League of Nations. This support provoked uproar, especially from Ramsay McDonald, the Prime Minister.

The whole thing did Bartlett's career a power of no good. The BBC would no longer support him as a broadcaster and he took on a far less prestigious job with the *News Chronicle*. However, he again surprised everyone. In 1938 he stood as an Independent in a Bridgwater by-election and although he had no party to give him assistance, he succeeded in winning what had always been a safe Tory seat. He remained an M.P. until 1950.

During the Second World War Bartlett again put his broadcasting expertise to great use with a thrice-weekly programme called 'Postscript'. These talks were delivered with passion, but also tempered by humour, and they did much to sustain the country's high wartime morale.

Once, at a Kremlin dinner, Bartlett responded to the toast, 'The Press' and took the opportunity to tell his Russian hosts, very politely, that without a free press people would always be slaves. Joe Stalin commented for all to hear: 'That young man talks too much.'

Later in life, Vernon Bartlett travelled widely and devoted himself to more general writing, including his autobiography, 'This is my Life'. An aspect of Vernon Bartlett's career is that, together with R.C. Sherriff, he wrote the novel version of Sherriff's play, 'Journeys End'. However, the novel did not enjoy anywhere near the enormous success of the play. Vernon Bartlett died in Yeovil in 1983.

R.G. Worcester (W 1931-1935) specialised in writing about aviation. He learnt to fly whilst still at Blundell's and on leaving he attended the Airspeed School of Aeronautical Engineering. During the war he served as a pilot with the R.N.V.R.

It was when he started writing for *Aeroplane Magazine*, specialising in reports on new aircraft, that he began to make a name for himself as someone who couldn't stand the sycophancy of the aviation trade press. He then started up his own publication, *Aviation Report*. This was published twice a week, had no advertising, no pictures, was produced entirely by himself, and cost an incredible £10 a copy. Worcester's main argument, made repeatedly in his magazine, was that the industry was wasting public money on too many ill-considered and non competitive projects, such as the TSR2.

Eventually, with aviation costs soaring, the government asked Worcester to advise them. This led to the cancellation of the TSR2 and the rationalisation of the industry into two main companies, BAC and Hawker Siddeley. In 1957 Worcester published a report called, 'An Industry Gone Mad'. But not all of his doom-laden prophesies turned out to be accurate.

He published his last *Aviation Report* in 1999 at the age of 82, having written around 14 million words on aviation. He died in 2003 aged 86.

Jon Swain (FH) spent a comparatively short time at Blundell's in the 1960s and it was not regarded as a happy encounter by either side. Once he had left, he embarked upon a life of extraordinary adventures. First, he joined the French Foreign Legion for traditional reasons, but unlike Beau Geste he soon opted out in favour of journalism, starting in Paris and then moving on to the far east, notably Vietnam and Cambodia. Starting as a freelance, he produced such fresh and evocative reports that he was soon signed up as a regular war correspondent for *The Sunday Times*.

Throughout the period of the Vietnam and Cambodian conflicts he remained at the heart of the wars. He was an integral part of the horrendous 'Killing Fields' and never flinched from dangers, thus enabling him to paint an alarmingly true picture of what was going on. This culminated, some years later, in his acclaimed book, 'River of Time'. This is far more than a story of wars: it is his personal story as well, a moving description as to how he fell in love with Vietnam and also a beautiful woman named Jacqueline. What also comes across is that in an odd, indefinable way, he fell in love with the war. He found all the death and destruction to be a siren call he just could not resist. Swain has always been a restless spirit and in 'River of Time' he is utterly candid about his own shortcomings; but however abrasive he appears to be as an individual, he is certainly a journalist and prose writer of very rare talent, some would say the greatest war reporter since Ernie Pyle and Alan Moorhead. The manner in which Swain captures the weird, frightening, and yet fascinating, atmosphere of war-torn Vietnam is probably only surpassed by Graham Greene's 'The Quiet American'.

Robert Fox (OH 1959-63) is a war and foreign correspondent of a very different type, being far more conventional. After leaving Blundell's he went up to Magdalen College, Oxford and from there he joined the BBC as a producer before becoming a general news reporter. He has, for a long time, been a regular contributor to the *Daily Telegraph*.

As a reporter he has covered a remarkable range of events, from Northern Ireland to terrorist outbreaks and earthquakes and natural disasters all over the world. In 1982 he won a Churchill Fellowship to study community radio and television in remote areas. He is, perhaps, best known for his coverage of the Falklands War, being one of the first ashore at the San Carlos beachhead. He then 'yomped' across the island to be in at the kill at Port Stanley, without ever indulging in the false bravado so beloved by journalists such as Max Hastings and John Simpson. Fox's book on the Falklands campaign, 'Eyewitness Falklands' was much admired and widely read.

Robert Fox later went on to cover the United Nations Desert Storm operation in Iraq, being attached to the 14th/20th King's Hussars, one of the armoured regiments in the thick of things. Robert Fox has been awarded the MBE for his reporting services and remains one of Britain's most highly respected journalists, the type of scribe to whom the more discerning readers turn when they want to know what is really happening in the latest world 'hot-spot'.

As already mentioned, journalism covers a vast field which means there are far too many Old Blundellian journalists to mention in this short survey. Representative of this profession, however, are such men as **Derek Rowles (NC 1949-1952)**, a specialist freelance writer who has concentrated on local history; **Christopher Jaques (OH 1970-1975)** who has contributed to Sunday paper supplements; **Mark Hollands (OH 1976-1977)**, who, after starting on the *Sidmouth Herald*, became foreign news editor of Australia's top daily paper, *The Australian* based in Sydney; and **Gordon Spurway (NC 1938-1941)** who had varied experience on numerous papers and periodicals in what used to be Rhodesia. Another Old Blundellian, **Orlando Murrin (FH 1971-1975)**, has for many years had a successful career in glossy magazines, very often ladies' glossies.

A man who defies any easy classification (and who I have therefore earmarked as an eccentric journalist), is **Don Manley (M 1958-63)**. He specialises in making up crossword puzzles. He started as a scientist, then became a commissioning editor in the Education Division of Oxford University Press. Later on, he went to Blackwells to specialise in school text books. Finally, after more years of a scientific nature, he settled, in October 2002, for being a crossword setter and freelance editor. So those of you who regularly cheat by using your special crossword dictionaries whilst trying to do cryptic crosswords in *The Radio Times*, the *Listener*, the *Independent on Sunday*, *The Times*, the *Guardian*, and *The Financial Times*, might just as well give Don Manley a buzz on the telephone (or e-mail!) and save yourselves a lot of time.

MEMOIRS, BIOGRAPHY, AND HISTORY

A Blundell's headmaster who always attracts praise – nothing but praise – is the Reverend Neville Gorton, who went on from Blundell's to become Bishop of Coventry. His years at Blundell's, from 1934-1942, are covered with rare skill and thoroughness by **Sir John Margetson (OH 1941-45)** in his biography 'Gorty'. In this delightful book, Sir John emphasises how a lovable and eccentric visionary transformed Blundell's and created a new attitude towards education which all successful public schools have, to one degree or another, followed; what you might call a modern Dr. Arnold. Yet Sir John Margetson makes it clear that in today's climate 'Gorty' would never have stood a chance of becoming a headmaster; and here, surely, is an overriding lesson, or message, which we will ignore at our peril. 'Gorty' illustrates that there is far more to education than passing exams, and to be a successful head teacher a man (or a woman) must be able to inspire pupils by dint of personality and personal example.

Sir John Margetson is well qualified to write 'Gorty'. He was not only a pupil at Blundell's during his headmastership, but, in the course of a highly successful diplomatic career, has taken a deep interest in education generally. For many years he has been Chairman of the Governors at a very large international school in the Netherlands, and also in the smaller, but just as prestigious, Yehudi Menuhin School in England.

'Gorty' has had lavish praise in all quarters, but especially from Chris Woodhouse, the ex-Chief Inspector of Schools, writing in the *Sunday Telegraph*.

Going back in time, to 1905, well before Gorty so unexpectedly wove his magic, and when Blundell's had a reputation as a 'rough and tumble' school, **M.L. Banks (Master 1889-1892)** was an assistant master. To celebrate the 300th anniversary of the school, he brought out a book entitled, 'Blundell's Worthies' and this has been used by all and sundry ever since as a guide to the success of the school. Now, in our 400th year, **E.R. Crowe (FH 1943-45)** is about to repeat a similar exercise, bringing 'Blundell's Worthies' up to date.

F.J. Snell (1877-1881) was one of Blundell's most prolific authors with a loyal and enormously wide readership. To illustrate this point, my copy of his best known work, 'Blundell's', was purchased at a second hand book shop in the Blue Mountains, Australia; and when the exorbitant price of $55 was queried, the bookseller (a Digger suitably attired in shorts and a cork-bespangled bush hat), responded with impressive authority, "No go, mate. What you've got there is bloody literature. . . scholarship. . . all about toffs, the bloody stuck-up Poms!'

Snell's many books covered a wide range of subjects, being particularly interested in local history and such places as Exmoor.

When it comes to a more recent account of Blundell's, the ex-head of the History Department, and currently the School archivist, **Charles Noon (1972-2003)**, has had published a handsomely illustrated book which mentions as many notable Blundellians as possible. He is also the author of 'Jack Russell' the famous Old Blundellian from Exmoor who founded the Jack Russell breed of dog, and after whom the school cross-country race, held every spring term, is named.

A Blundell's master who published a very distinguished biography is **Brian Jenkins (Master 1965-91)**. This was 'Citizen Daniel: the Call of America – early correspondence of the Constables of Horley'. This book came about by the Constable family accidentally donating to the school the papers of a distant cousin, Sir Robert Blundell. Brian Jenkins soon realised the historical significance of the papers and produced a biography which gives a fascinating insight into America in the late eighteenth and early nineteenth centuries.

Jenkins has also been published on matters nearer to home, namely 'The Removal of Blundell's 1846-1882', which was written to celebrate a hundred years of Blundell's at Horsdon. He still hopes to resume work on a comprehensive history of Blundell's.

A colleague of Brian Jenkins was **D.H. Japes (Master 1966-1995)**. He attended Exeter College, Oxford and in 1992 published a definitive biography of William Payne, the Plymouth artist. **D.G.O. Ayerst (Master 1934-1938)** was another history master. He broke into print shortly after leaving Blundell's just before the Second World War. His best known work is 'Biography of a Newspaper', a 600 page history of the *Guardian*. For many years he worked for the *Guardian* and was regarded as one of its leading journalists.

War invariably features in many memoirs. One book, concerning his days as a prisoner of war under the Japanese, was written by **Lt Colonel R. Burton (OH 1929-1931)**. Burton has an extraordinary story to tell. He was wounded in the closing stages of the disastrous defence of Singapore, and he then went on to suffer the very worst the Japanese could hand out in the way of torture, starvation, and general maltreatment. Somehow, Burton survived, which many of his comrades didn't, of course. Later, when he came to write his story (which he entitled 'The Road to Three Pagodas') he had great difficulty in finding a publisher. Russell Braddon had already hit the best-seller list with 'Naked Island' and it was assumed that the market had been satisfied. It hadn't, of course, but when Burton eventually found a publisher he was forced, as a serving army officer, to submit his manuscript to the War Office for vetting. They objected to numerous passages because they might offend the Japanese. It was pointed out to Burton that the Japanese were now our allies and trading partners and they might think his comments represented the view of the British Army.

Consequently, although 'The Road to Three Pagodas' duly came out (minus the offending passages), Burton could not wait until he was out of the army and free to write what he liked. He then produced the full, true version with no holds barred, under the title 'Railway to Hell'.

Even though Colonel Burton handles his subject with calmness and dignity, it is not a pleasant read; but it is a read which should be compulsory for all young people. What happened should not be forgotten: forgiven, maybe; but never forgotten. Tragically, Lt Colonel Burton, who lived locally at Newton Abbott, died very recently.

Another young man who went through what many people would regard as 'hell' was, **Sir John Palmer (Chairman of Governors 1980-92)**. Of course, Sir John, being the mild and mannerly gentleman that he was, made it look far more bearable than it really was, and the title of his book 'Luck on my Side' is typically low key. When the war started he had just come down from Oxford so he immediately joined the Royal Navy Volunteer Reserve. He then spent most of his time on convoy work, both in the Atlantic and the Mediterranean. The book not only portrays the horrors of war at sea, but paints a vivid picture of how the young men of those days were able to take such things in their stride. After the war he qualified as a solicitor and became President of the Law Society. He also died very recently.

A man with a remarkable military distinction is **W.G. Jenkins (DB 1938-42).** As a young subaltern, fighting in the northern Italy campaign, he was awarded a DSO, as opposed to the normal gallantry award for that rank, a Military Cross. This information comes out in Jenkins's book 'Commando Subaltern at War'. He starts by telling us a little about his schooldays at Blundell's and then he launches into a riveting account of his days in the Royal Marine Commandos. First he went into Yugoslavia to help Tito and his partisans. Then they switched their support to Mihailovic and soon they came to realise the utter confusion, internal feuds, and conflicts of loyalty which prevailed in Yugoslavia in those days. There were Fascist Croats, Royalist Serbs, Communists, Anarchists, and more than a fair share of outright brigands who would cut anyone's throat for the price of a fag. In fact, by reading Jenkins's book, one gets the impressions that things were much the same then as they are now.

Jenkins was lucky in as much that, before long, he joined 43 Commando and concentrated on independent raids on the German held Dalmatian islands. In early 1945 Jenkins was posted to northern Italy and he gives a graphic account of the Eighth Army's Spring Offensive. It was during a prolonged action around the River Reno, just west of Argenta, that Jenkins won his DSO.

After the war, Jenkins became a lecturer at RMA Sandhurst and assisted with Adventure Training and military exercises.

David Godfrey (FH 1940-1942) concentrates on more pleasant things in his book of memoirs entitled, 'Reckoning with the Force'. Not that there is anything easy and straight forward about being a special branch police officer in Jamaica in the days before independence; but Godfrey looks on the humorous side of things, producing hilarious stories all of which have the ring of truth about them.

On leaving Blundell's Godfrey served in the navy in the far east and went to Jamaica aged twenty-three, so it's really no surprise that in his book he manages to convey the spirit which existed in the West Indies in the latter days of colonialism. Godfrey says he's now bitten by the writing bug so, hopefully, there will soon be more of his delightful tales.

In a similar way, **J.S.H. Cunyngham-Brown (NC 1920-1924)** relied on his personal experiences to give us an amusing and exciting book entitled, 'Tales from the South China Seas', based on his job as a civil servant in Malaysia before and after the Second World War. On leaving Blundell's Cunyngham-Brown abandoned ideas of a medical profession in order to go to sea and he was one of the deck hands on the *William Mitchell* when it completed its service as one of the last grain clippers. Then, in 1929, he joined the Malayan civil service. He served in Penang and later in Singapore and Jahore as a magistrate and controller of labour. In the war, he had many adventures with the RNVR. He ferried refugees to Sumatra and got into all kinds of trouble when he tried to sail an outrigger to Ceylon. He was captured by the Japanese and sentenced to death. Only the end of hostilities saved him. After the war, he remained in Penang and became a legendary figure. He died in Georgetown in 1989 aged 83.

Sticking to war memoirs, we come across Blundell's greatest warrior, a bold claim by the writer of these notes when there are people like Major-General Gracey (the unsung hero of India/Pakistan separation) to compete with. However, the career of **General Sir Walter Walker KCB OBE DSO (and two bars) PSNB, (DB 1926-1931)** does put him in a class of his own. In 1978 he wrote his first book 'The Bear at the Back Door' and in 1980 his second, 'The Next Domino'. His third and final book 'Fighting On' stands supreme among them. In it, he writes with military precision, in the mode of an operations order, and there's not much he doesn't tell us with complete candour.

Candour, straight-dealing, and plain language were the hallmark of the man and they made him a firm favourite with the men he commanded. He also had a unique talent for appreciating a situation and the imagination to devise tactics

General Walker

accordingly. Hence it is no surprise when he claims (quite correctly, most military men are agreed) that his campaign in the secretive 'war' against Indonesia in Borneo was a text book example of how to achieve victory in the face of hostile superiors. The prospect of upsetting politicians and the CIGS never daunted Walter Walker. If he knew he was right, he'd take on anyone. He had complete faith in his own judgement and having determined on a course of action he stuck to it until he achieved it, no matter how many feathers were ruffled in the process.

Despite his unpopularity in high places, General Walker's abilities could not be denied and he was eventually appointed Commander-in-Chief, Allied Forces Northern Europe. When he left the army, General Walker became gravely concerned with the state of the country under a socialist government. He led several notable figures in forming an organisation which he called 'Civil Assistance'. This was designed to give the country new leadership and to rejuvenate the country so that it would no longer be regarded as the 'sick man' of Europe. As things turned out, the total political collapse that seemed likely never came; but Walter Walker would have been ready.

His latter years were tragically marred by botched hip operations and he spent several years in great pain. For such a brilliant man, who had fought so hard for peace and security, it was a cruel end to an honourable career.

General Walker would have been the first to acknowledge that the survival of our country during two world wars depended, more than anything else, on the bravery and dedication of those who did the actual fighting. This comes across very clearly in a book by **Hugh Lynch-Blosse (Petergate 1931-1935)**, 'Wings – and Other Things'. This book covers a lot of ground, from his happy school days at Blundell's, through Cranwell, and then on to his career in the R.A.F., in which he ended as a Group Captain with an OBE. During the early days of the war he served in 104, 110, and 40 Squadrons, the last two on operations in 1940 and early 1941. Those were frantic and very dangerous days and whilst Lynch-Blosse was on a raid over Berlin his aircraft was so badly damaged that he and his crew had to bail out, all of them spending the rest of the war in various prisoner-of-war camps.

The book also deals with the post-war period and gives a touching account of his happy family life, with his son, David, following him into Petergate. General Walker's younger brother, Harold, (a distinguished gynaecologist) was a close school friend of Lynch-Blosse's and when he reviewed 'Wings – and Other Things' he concluded: 'A good read. A magnum opus. Buy it.'

R.A.W. Rudd (M and SH 1938-1942) was another Old Blundellian who ended up 'in the bag'. He was likewise shot-down over Germany. His book, 'One Boy's War' was written because of Rudd's awareness of the gulf opening up between the generations, and the need for younger people to understand what others sacrificed for their freedom. Rudd was born in South Africa and after the war continued his education at Oxford University. After working as a financial journalist for the *Manchester Guardian* he set up his own stockbroking company in 1969. He retired from active business when he became handicapped by poor eyesight and now lives in London.

Major Tim Owen R.M. (NC 1933-1938) was another Old Blundellian who saw military service during World War II, being an interpreter; but the book he has recently had published, 'Beyond the Empty Quarter', concentrates on his experiences after the war, in the Middle East, principally the Sultanate of Oman between 1957 and 1998.

In Oman, everything revolves around oil and Tim Owen deals with its discovery and the developments that followed. Yet Owen also gives us a brilliantly clear idea of what that country was like before oil transformed it: a country blighted by poverty, with a strictly nomadic culture.

For a time Tim Owen worked for Shell, but when he left them in 1969 he continued to visit Oman and his recollections include the period immediately after the internal coup of 1970 when the present Sultan snatched power from his father. In his long association with the Middle East and all its weird contradictions and false values, Tim Owen was also a free-lance journalist, contributing regularly to the *Financial Times*, the *Economist*, and other leading publications.

If, as the writer of these notes, I was asked to name my favourite among 'Blundellian' books, 'Portrait of an Architect' by **Raglan Squire (SH 1926-1930)** would be around the top, among the much more famous contenders. Raglan was, of course, the son of Sir John Squire, and in my estimation that gives him a head start. Not that there seems to be much similarity between father and son. Sir John (as I've mentioned) was the world's worst cricketer, whereas Raglan was a very fine one. He was also a rugby player of repute; hardly the forte of his father, I would think.

After Blundell's Raglan Squire went up to Cambridge and eventually became an architect. He set up on his own in 1937, soon to be interrupted by the war years when he served with distinction in 'the Sappers'. In his autobiography, Raglan describes how his work took him all over the world; but what comes out of his book are not so much the hotels he built, or the housing estates, or the offices or factories, or the five Hilton Hotels scattered across the world, but rather the man himself, his zest for life, his sense of humour and fun: a man who enjoyed life to the full. He contributed to society enormously, and he always managed to maintain the standards he had learnt in his childhood and schooldays. Sadly, he died very recently.

Raglan Squire

SCIENCE AND MEDICINE

Over its 400 years of existence Blundell's has made great contributions to science and medicine. Towering above all others is **Professor A.V. Hill (DB 1900-1905)**. He won a scholarship to Blundell's and was an outstanding mathematician, studying under J.M.Thornton. From Blundell's he went up to Trinity College, Cambridge, and then, under the influence of L.M. Fletcher and Sir F.G. Hopkins, he turned to physiology.

Professor Hill is the only Blundellian to have won the Nobel Prize. This was for his work in connection with muscular movement, with the Prize being given in 1923 when Hill held the chair of Physiology at Manchester University. However, it says much for Hill's versatility as a scientist that some of his most important work – which had a far more immediate and vital impact than his work on muscles – was the development of the country's radar system, which he masterminded in conjunction with Lord Blackett and Sir H.T. Tizard.

From 1940 to 1945 Professor Hill was the Independent Member of Parliament for Cambridge University and he went on numerous important overseas missions on behalf of the

Professor A.V. Hill (middle)

government. In 1943-44 he visited India to advise on post-war reconstruction, with special emphasis on medical education. Throughout his career, Hill held many distinguished fellowships yet he still found time to write numerous learned papers and books, such as 'Adventures in Biophysics'; 'Chemical Wave Transmission in Nerve'; 'Trails and Trial on Physiology'; and 'The Ethical Dilemma of Science'.

A.V. Hill combined intensive research work in the laboratory with a remarkable dedication to public service. He edited the journal of the British Physiological Society and he was in at the foundation of the Academic Assistance Council, an organisation that helped scientists experiencing hard times or distress. In particular, he did great work in helping scientists hounded out of Europe by Hitler. He was also noted for his friendliness and willingness to help his junior colleagues. He died in 1977 at Cambridge.

Morris William Travers went to Blundell's when he was only twelve but he straight away showed an aptitude for science and won the fifth form prize for chemistry. After Blundell's he went to the University College, London, and received a degree in Chemistry in 1893. Shortly afterwards he worked on the properties of the newly discovered gas, Helium, with a book entitled 'Experimental Study of Gases', published in 1901. Other discoveries concerning gases followed and he published further books entitled: 'The Discovery of the Rare Gases' (1928); and 'A Life of Sir William Ramsey' in 1956.

During his career, Travers was instrumental in taking the University College in Bristol to full university status and around the same time he travelled to India as director of the proposed Institute of Science at Bangalore. During World War I, Travers was involved in important work concerning the use of glass. Similar work cropped up again during the second world war, this time with explosives added to his responsibilities.

The exposure of the Piltdown Man as a fake, which caused a tremendous controversy and furore in Britain in 1953, was mainly due to an Old Blundellian, **Sir Wilfred Le Gros Clark NC 1910-1912)**. His sensational findings that this so-called prehistoric man was an utter fraud (made in conjunction with Weiner and Oakley) were published in the *Bulletin of the British Museum*.

When Le Gros Clark first went to Blundell's his progress was hampered by a bad stammer, but he later overcame this handicap. Just before World War I he attended St Thomas's Hospital where both his grandfathers had served with distinction. When war broke out, Clark joined the R.A.M.C.

Five years later he went to Sarawak as principal medical officer. When he eventually returned to England he was appointed Professor of Anatomy at Oxford, a post he occupied until his retirement in 1962.

Le Gros Clark's first book was on man's evolution, 'Early Forerunners of Man', and then followed six short books on Australopithecines and a handbook for the British Museum, 'History of the Primates'. He also wrote a host of articles and papers and an autobiographical book, 'Chant of Pleasant Exploration', published in 1968.

His knighthood was bestowed on him in 1955 and over the years he gained a host of awards and distinctions, including being made an Honorary Fellow of Hertford College, Oxford, in 1962. He died in June 1971 whilst staying with friends in Dorset.

Dr. David Hay (P 1944-1949) is a lover of books. He puts so much store on their value that when he and his elder brother **Andrew Hay (P 1942-45)** took an early look at the newly opened Blundell's library, they were so aghast that the books were very nearly outnumbered by computers that they immediately donated a very handsome sum for the purchase of new books; and what a difference it has made!

David Hay is not only interested in books, but he is also a dab hand at writing them. Recently he has published a specialised book entitled: 'A Flickering Lamp: A History of the Sydenham Medical Club (1775-200)'. The Club could best be described as an exclusive doctors' club in London. Over the years it has numbered many famous names among its members. This is a work of detailed research and recounts its early history and how its name was changed in 1912 from The Monday Medical Club to the Sydenham Club in memory of the father of English clinical medicine, Thomas Sydenham.

David Hay describes the members of the Club against the changing background of London. The Club comes across as a delightful, if somewhat eccentric and well lubricated, relic of

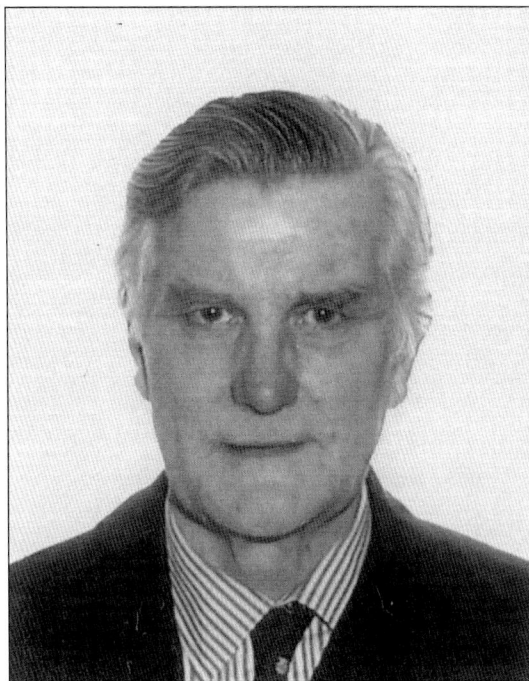

Dr. David Hay

the past. Robin Fox, editor of *The Journal of the Royal Society of Medicine*, takes a dim view of this and in his review of the book, says: 'The Club and its survival might also be of interest to anthropologists'. It sounds to the writer of these notes as though Robin Fox would have benefited from a few turbulent, politically incorrect, years in Petergate in its heyday!

The book is well illustrated and has a foreword by Sir Richard Bayliss.

Dr. Bob Bowles (NC 1943-1947) is another doctor who has broken into print as a consequence of his medical career. Like all pupils at Blundell's in the forties, Bob Bowles did well to survive the winter of '47 and progress to St Thomas's Hospital where he qualified. For some thirty years he was a GP in Lyme Regis, where he still lives. He retired in 1989. He then embarked on a new career as a medical writer. Quite apart from a long list of books, articles, and contributions to an impressive array of learned journals, Bob Bowles is also an accomplished public speaker and is much in demand.

One of his most impressive articles is a series in *Practice* entitled, 'Accuracy in Recording Practice Expenses'. Somehow I don't think that would have been top of the agenda at one of the early meetings of Dr. Hay's Monday Medical Club. Such is progress.

CEM Joad

POLITICS, PHILOSOPHY, CLASSICS, AND RELIGION

It is probable that more people have heard of Blundell's because of **Professor C.E.M. Joad** than any other individual. He was a very famous man indeed, one of the first of what can be described as a 'media star'. Practically all adults were acutely aware of him and millions of people hurried home to their wireless sets in order not to miss him on the famous 'Brains Trust' programme. He was a brilliant communicator and he had an ideal 'sidekick' in Commander Campbell, a man who differed from Joad in every way. The two of them held the country spellbound for the best part of a decade.

Joad could well have been the founder of 'catch phrases'. Whenever he was confronted by a tricky question he would play for time, by saying, 'Well, it depends what you mean by. . .' Soon, half the nation was using this as a let-out for their ignorance.

Joad went to Blundell's from the Dragon School, Oxford, and, after a dazzling time in the classrooms of Blundell's, he left in 1910 to go up to Balliol College, Oxford, to study philosophy. Having been the most brilliant scholar of his time at both Blundell's and Balliol, he surprised everyone by joining the labour exchange department of the Board of Trade.

This was an odd choice for such a brilliant academic, but he no doubt made the right decision because his main interest was writing and whilst working as a civil servant he was able to spend most of his time producing a steady stream of books. They were mainly on political and philosophical subjects. In 1930 he left the Board of Trade and became head of the department of philosophy at Birkbeck College, University of London, a post he held until his death.

After philosophy, Joad's greatest interest was politics, and his life was dominated by his socialist and pacifist beliefs. His arch enemy in Britain from the 1930s onwards was Winston Churchill. The two men could not stand each other. The feud started when Joad organised a debate at the Oxford Union with the notorious motion that 'This House is not prepared to fight for King and Country'. Joad did not speak in the debate but it was well known that he was the inspiration behind the motion and when it was carried handsomely the repercussions were startling. It is said that Hitler was so impressed by this vote of Britain's finest young men that he was convinced Britain would never have the stomach to resist his various adventures. Hence, Churchill's contempt for Joad.

Joad put his socialist principles to work in various other ways. He often spoke at the Fabian Society and was a leading light in the Workers' Education Association. He also had a deep love of the countryside and was a guide in various rambling and climbing clubs.

It was during the war that he came to prominence as a broadcaster in 'Brains Trust' and his popularity led many people, from all walks of life, to take an interest in philosophy and its history. His great success was due to his ability to explain things in simple terms. He became the champion of many losing causes. In 1948 he published 'Decadence' in which he dealt with the evils of the times.

Joad was something of an eccentric in his mode of dress and was a man of boundless energy, splitting his time between London and his farm in Hampshire. However, his entire career suddenly collapsed in a sad and nonsensical manner. He was convicted of travelling on a train without a ticket and overnight everyone turned against him. Even the Old Blundellian Club expelled him. What very few of these critics realised was that Joad had a rather childish tendency towards practical jokes and stunts, and one of his amusements was to see how far he could get on the trains by only using platform tickets. It was, to him, rather like undergraduates stealing policemen's helmets: wrong but harmless. The railway police were aware of his antics but there came a time when they decided to throw the book at him. His conviction not only ruined his career but many said hastened his death.

He wrote nearly fifty books throughout his career. His last one was 'The Recovery of Belief' in 1952, by which time he was already suffering from cancer with death approaching.

Another Old Blundellian socialist (although of a very different hue to Joad), was **Michael Shanks (SH 1939-45)**. He was more interested in international business and economics than philosophy; what you might call a practical socialist. From Blundell's he too went to Balliol, a residency that was split in two for he did his military service as a 2nd Lt in the Artillery before returning to Balliol for an additional degree.

In 1951 he went to the States to lecture on economics and then, when he returned to Britain, he contributed both 'leaders' and feature articles for the *Financial Times*. Whatever his job, he always travelled extensively, particularly in Europe and the States. With his reputation growing rapidly, he was soon doing a lot of radio and television work. He also had consultancy jobs with Granada Television and Penguin Books and in 1965 he became economics correspondent for *The Sunday Times*. At the same time, he took on a second career, that of industrial policy adviser and co-ordinator to the Labour Government.

Yet another change of direction came when he was appointed economics adviser to British Leyland, helping another Old Blundellian, Lord Stokes, to create British Leyland Motors. He was only there a short time before he moved to British Oxygen where he became chief executive.

All this time, his writing output never slackened and he produced several very highly rated books, including, 'The Stagnant Society'; 'Lessons of Public Enterprise'; 'The Innovators'; 'The Quest for Growth; 'Planning and Politics'; and 'What's Wrong With the Modern World?'.

Shanks was very much an internationalist. He made the welfare of black workers for BOC in South Africa a personal concern. He was also a keen European and in 1973 was appointed as one of the four British directors-general in charge of employment and social affairs.

Shanks was a man of enormous energy, but many felt his career would have been far more effective if he had been more settled in his outlook; but as it was he was taken ill whilst still relatively young and died in a Sheffield Hospital. If he had enjoyed a normal life-span, there is no knowing what he would have achieved.

There are some human beings who are destined to be flung into a situation where their advice or actions influence the lives of millions, even change the course of history. Churchill was such a man, of course, and so too (in a lesser degree) was his Air Minister in 1940, **Lord Balfour of Inchrye (SH 1913-1914)**. It was on to Lord Balfour's desk in the Air Ministry that Air Chief Marshal Dowding (Commander-in-Chief, Fighter Command) dropped his famous memo to Churchill, urging him to break his promise to the French and retain all Fighter Command's Spitfires in England for the coming Battle of Britain. Balfour was left as the middleman and it was due (at least in part) to his advice to heed Dowding's warning that Churchill broke his promise and abandoned any further air support for the French: a vital factor in the victory of the

Lord Balfour of Inchrye

Battle of Britain, probably the most decisive battle in modern history, certainly since Waterloo.

Lord Balfour arrived at Blundell's late in his school career. He had previously been to BRNC Dartmouth but left there on deciding to abandon plans for a naval career. He was so keen on flying that he borrowed £75 from his father, Field Marshal Lord Napier of Magdda, in order to take lessons. When World War I broke out he managed to get into the Royal Flying Corps and he had a distinguished flying career. He shot down eleven enemy aircraft and won a Military Cross and Bar in recognition of his exploits. Not that it was all glory: Balfour was lucky to survive what became known in his unit as 'Bloody April' in which they lost 35 pilots and observers.

At 21 Balfour was promoted to Major and when the war ended he went to Cranwell as an instructor. In 1923 he left the RAF and pursued a career as a journalist and a politician. After one abortive attempt to unseat a labour member in a safe seat, he was elected to Parliament for The Isle of Thanet in 1929. He then became Parliamentary Secretary of State for Air in 1938, a post he held until 1944.

In this critical job he not only influenced the decision on abandoning the French, but he was right at the centre of the feud between Air Marshals Park and Leigh-Mallory about the use of 'Big Wings', a dispute never satisfactorily resolved.

After the war, Lord Balfour was sent by Churchill to be Resident Minister in West Africa. When he returned he was created Baron Balfour of Inchrye and took his seat in the House of Lords. Throughout this period Balfour retained his interest in journalism and he also wrote a sequel to his first book, 'An Airman Marches'. This second book, which sold in large numbers, was 'Wings Over Westminster'. He also wrote a more relaxed book entitled, 'Fish, Folk, and Fun,' which reflected his lifelong passion for fly-fishing. He died aged 90.

Turning rather abruptly from politics to religion, **Philip McNair (DB 1937-1941)** is a Blundellian who has a fine reputation as a Renaissance historian. After leaving Blundell's, he went on to gain degrees at both Oxford and Cambridge and has held several prestigious posts, including Dean of Darwin College, Cambridge, and Serena Professor of Italian in the University of Birmingham. His latest book is 'Patterns of Perfection' which highlights seven Sermons preached in Patria by Bernardino Ohino in the 16th century. He is also author of studies on St. Francis of Assisi, Dante, Petrarch, Poliziano and others. He has also written on the Turin Shroud and aspects of 19th century religious history.

One of the greatest virtues of Neville Gorton as a headmaster was his ability to attract the finest staff. When, in 1942, a certain **Professor S H Hooke** was bombed out in London, leaving his wife distraught, Gorty invited the professor (an old friend) to get away from the dangers of London by teaching at Blundell's

Hooke, although principally a theologian, was a man of such great versatility that he had no trouble turning his hand to teaching a wide range of subjects to the Classical Sixth. He was slow to settle into Blundell's, mainly because the boys could hardly credit his wide range of knowledge. They were also suspicious of his curious dress (loud plus fours) and the way he was eternally lighting and re-lighting his beloved pipe. He soon won them over with his sense of humour. This was sparked off when a boy asked him, "Please, sir. Who is this bloke Ibid?" This howler gave rise to a secret 'Ibid Club', confined to the classical Sixth which used to meet in Hooke's bungalow.

One of Professor Hooke's many claims to literary fame is his translation of the Bible. He managed to do a lot of writing whilst at Blundell's and he would very often try out his efforts on the boys, chapter by chapter, as they rolled off his 'conveyor belt'.

Hooke lived to the ripe old age of 93 and during this time he collected a list of academic honours and appointments which is far too long to catalogue here. Suffice to say that he was one of the greatest religious and biblical scholars of his generation. Among his best known books are 'The Bible in Basic English'; 'Middle Eastern Mythology'; 'Alpha and Omega'; 'In the Beginning' and 'The Siege Perilous'. A remarkable teacher and an even more remarkable man.

The irony of Professor Hooke's time at Blundell's is that when Gorty left to become Bishop of Coventry, his successor, the Rev R L Roberts, was so envious of Hooke's knowledge, reputation, and his success with the boys, that he found an excuse to sack him. Never mind 'The Man who Shot Liberty Vallence'; far more incredible is 'The Man who Sacked Professor Hooke!'

Professor George Huxley (SH 1946-50) was an outstanding classics scholar at Blundell's and most people assumed (correctly) that he would progress to great academic distinction. From Blundell's he went up to Magdalen College Oxford and got a 1st in Greats. He then became Fellow of All Souls College, Oxford, 1955-61, and during his illustrious career has held a whole host of appointments invariably founded on the basis of ancient Greece. His entry in 'Who's Who' is (thanks to the ridiculously small print) a bewildering array of appointments and distinctions which come and go and overlap. Of his publications there are no doubts, however. He is author of, 'Achaens and Hittites': 'Early Sparta'; 'The Early Ionians'; 'Greek Epic Poetry from Eumelo to Panyassis'; 'Pindar's Vision of the Past'; 'On Aristotle and Greek Society'; and 'Homer and the Travellers'. His recreation is listed as 'Siderodromophilia.' The writer of these notes was a contemporary of George Huxley and I remember him above all as a 'trainiac' with his first venture into print, whilst still in SH, being a fascinating account of the Tivvy Bumper.

Back now to religion, and this survey comes to two very famous man who, in the strictest sense, were not Blundellians, yet they were men who were so closely involved with Blundell's, and contributed so much to the school, with a truly enormous impact on pupils, that I have decided to

Bishop Stockwood

include them anyhow. Now that there are such people as Honorary Old Blundellians (they were created in 2003), I hereby take it upon myself, with no authority whatsoever, to declare **The Rt Rev. Mervyn Stockwood & The Rt Reverend John Robinson, (Bishops of Southwark and Woolwich respectively)** to be our first posthumous Honorary Old Blundellians.

Mervyn Stockwood was arguably the most controversial of all anglican bishops. When ordained he went as curate to Saint Matthew's, Moorfields, in Bristol, and so began his long association with Blundell's. From 1936 to 1941 he was the school's missioner. Those without any knowlege of the Blundell's mission in Bristol will have little idea of what a wonderful institution it was, nor how closely the mission and the school worked together. Robinson took over as missioner from Stockwood and both men were dedicated to their task. They visited the school at least once a week and stayed overnight, and throughout the time of the mission's existence competitive sports and camps were organised which enabled deprived Bristol mission boys and Blundellians to meet and get to know each other in a relaxed atmosphere, something that worked splendidly. Both Mervyn Stockwood and John Robinson preached at Blundell's frequently and Stockwood was a particularly warm friend of the headmaster, Gorty. The literary output of both men was prodigious, especially in religious journalism.

Perhaps the best known book of Mervyn Stockwood's was 'Chanctonbury Ring', published in 1982. Undoubtedly John Robinson's finest piece of writing was 'Honest to God', published in 1963. In that year alone it was reprinted four times and literally swept the country. Sales were only outstripped by the influence the book had, for it dared to question the entire religious framework upon which Christianity had hitherto been presented.

TRAVEL AND LEISURE

S.H. Burton (Master 1945-1964) was one in a long line of brilliant heads of the Blundell's English department. He is also one of the country's leading authorities on Exmoor. He knew the moor like the back of his hand and he had the delightful habit, once A level exams were over, of taking his 6th form pupils to the top of Dunkery Beacon where we discussed Shelley, Byron, and the rest of them, whilst admiring the view and eating curly Spam sandwiches, a speciality of the ex-RSM (ATS) caterer, Miss Talbot.

Sam Burton published other books on Devon and the West Country, notably 'The North Devon Coasts'; 'Lorna Doone Trail'; 'Coast of Cornwall'; and 'Devon Villages', but it is probable that, financially, he was more successful with his English text books. In the early fifties he brought out 'Criticism of Poetry' which was used by all Blundellian sixthformers, and I well remember Sam (he was also known as Tim) introducing it to us with the remark: 'And as far as I'm concerned you can destroy, mutilate, or lose, as many of these books as you like. The sooner there is a reprint, the better. . .'

*Christopher
Ondaatje*

After Sam left Blundell's in 1964 he went into Further Education and then veered in the direction of producing text books designed solely to help pupils swot their way through exams out of school hours: no doubt a vital and highly valuable contribution to the nation's education, but to the writer of these notes, it was a pity that he did not concentrate more on what I fancy was his first love, the glorious countryside of the West Country.

Another great admirer of the West Country is **Sir Christopher Ondaatje (P 1947-1951)**, yet his highly successful travel books are all set in very distant places. One is about his search for his roots in Sri Lanka, another concerns Richard Burton in the Sind, and then he takes us to Africa, first of all to look for a leopard in the afternoon, and then to check up on the source of the Nile, and finally to be reminded of what Ernest Hemingway got up to during his periodic visits to the dark continent. Perhaps the main attraction of all these books is the photography which, for the most part, Sir Christopher takes credit.

Ondaatje also published several other books whilst he was a resident of Canada, the most notable being 'Prime Ministers of Canada'. In recent years he has also become a patron of the arts. A handsome donation of £2.75 million was made for the extension of the National Portrait Gallery. He has also supported another great interest, cricket. He is Patron of the Somerset County Cricket Club as well as being a keen collector of cricket memorabilia. More recently he has set up a valuable literary prize (£10,000) to be awarded each year to the author who is most successful in evoking the atmosphere of a place. Ondaatje is a Fellow of the Royal Geographical Society, for whom he gives regular lectures. One wonders where Ondaatje's next travel book will be set. Back to Exmoor, perhaps?

Old Blundellians have never been backward in spreading themselves all around the globe, and one such is **David Fielding (FH 1948-1954)**. His stamping ground is Borneo and, with the help of his wife, he published in 1998 a fascinating book, with an abundance of illustrations, entitled, 'Borneo, Jewel in a Jade Rainbow'. The book takes us back to the early sixties to give a detailed look at the closing stages of colonialism. Sometimes it reads like a Noel Barber novel, with a terribly young British Administrator thrown into primitive conditions, and with his beautiful young wife saving the day during a cholera epidemic with her nursing skills.

More incidental (but just as fascinating) things happened to the young couple. Fielding recounts weird local customs, encounters with smugglers of illegal immigrants, details of pagan marriage ceremonies, and how he coped with long, drawn-out, drinking orgies in remote villages in the interior. Those were the days!

Tom Holden, a contemporary of Fielding's (who once had Idi Amin as his platoon sergeant in The King's African Rifles), reviewed the book and summed up by saying: 'A thoroughly good read.'

Clive Mumford (NC 1952-1957) chose the career of journalism when he left Blundell's, and he specialised in the West Country. Boxing was another of his interests and he was no mean exponent of the art of fisticuffs. He has also written travel books about a little known part of the world right on our doorstep, the Scilly Islands. The two best known are, 'Portrait of the Isles of Silly' and 'Scilly Peculiar, a Collection of the Comic and Curious'.

NATURE

Rev. David Quine (OH 1942-1947) had two major interests at Blundell's. Whilst more than holding his own academically, his undivided attention was gripped by his involvement in Blundell's sport (he was an OH Triple Colour), and his membership of the Bird Club, run by 'Bird' Reynolds. Pump Batterby and Quine's school friend Brian Tedd helped matters along and ever since those early days, right throughout university and a career as a school chaplain, David Quine has maintained his love of ornithology. He has published several books on his observations in the wild, notably 'St Kilda Revisited'; 'Island Guides'; 'St Kilda'; 'St Kilda Portraits'; and 'Life in Landale'. He has also written a host of articles for various magazines and periodicals. Complementing these things perfectly, he is a talented artist and photographer.

'Tarka the Otter' is a book most people have read and a book that can never be repeated or equalled. It is therefore not surprising that it has had an enormous influence on the life of **Richard Williamson (P 1949-1952)** one of the sons of the author, Henry Williamson. From his Blundell's days onwards, Williamson has been absorbed by the wonders of nature. At Blundell's the master who most influenced him was Joe Panther. This influence comes out clearly in his first

Richard Williamson

book, 'The Dawn is My Brother'. It deals with his days at Blundell's, then his years of national service in the Mediterranean and the Middle East.

Like so many writers, Richard Williamson usually had several things on the go at the same time. Whilst writing a wildlife column in the *Daily Mail* he was also working for the Forestry Commission. However, from 1963 until 1995 he served with the The Nature Conservancy Council as site manager for the Sussex nature reserves.

In 1972 Richard published 'Capreol, the Story of a Roebuck'; and in 1978 'The Great Yew Forest'. Film scripts and contributions towards television programmes followed over the years, to say nothing of extensive travel in Afghanistan and the Hindu Kush. For years now Williamson has been based in Sussex and in 1988 he was awarded an honorary MSc by the University of Chichester and West Sussex. He is still writing hard and has now turned towards novels with nature forming the backdrop and a main interest.

Captain C.R.S. Pitman (SH 1907-1908) had an interest in animals of a rather more exotic background to those that dominated the family writings of the Williamsons. Pitman started as a military man by going to the Officer Cadet School after Blundell's. In World War I he was then awarded the DSO and the MC whilst serving in Mesopotamia. He resigned his commission in 1921 in order to devote himself to the preservation of wild life. From 1925 to 1931 he was game warden for the Veanda Protectorate. He was then seconded to Northern Rhodesia for two years. He described many remarkable experiences with lions and other big game in two books, 'A Game Warden Among his Charges', and 'A Game Warden Takes Stock'.

Pitman then gained additional fame by writing three scientific books, 'A Guide to Snakes in Uganda'; 'Common Antelopes'; and 'Faunal Survey of Northern Rhodesia'. Pitman was elected a Scientific Fellow of the Zoological Society of London and was a member of many other zoological, ornithological, and naturalist Societies and Trusts all over the world. He was made a CBE in 1950 and died in London, aged 83, in 1975.

A CLASS OF THEIR OWN

This category should really be 'miscellaneous' but the above sounds so much more polite and flattering, and the fact is that the two authors who round off this survey of Blundell's writers do have a distinction all of their own, one because he is an expert in an aspect of life we have always taken for granted, with rarely a second thought, and the other because he writes books in Spanish as well as English, a language which the writer of these notes has conspicuously failed to master after twenty years of living in Tenerife, and whose admiration for such a feat therefore knows no bounds.

Dr. P. Woodward (OH 1932-1938) should really be best known as a scientist. He had a very distinguished career as one. At Blundell's he was an outstanding mathematician and musician.

He frequently played the organ in the chapel instead of Jazz Hall and he was also a leading member of Bundy Thomas's School Mathematics Team, although whether he got his 'Maths Socks' (coloured green, I believe) is not recorded. In the early days of the war, Woodward went to Wadham College, Oxford, and then became what in those days was known as a 'Boffin'. He worked in the development of radar and was very active in the early days of computers. At that time, if you wanted a computer you built it yourself.

He became a visiting professor at Harvard but most of his time has been spent in Malvern developing highly sophisticated computer software for the government. In 1980 Woodward retired and then concentrated upon his horological interests which had started in childhood. In 1995 Oxford University Press published his book 'My Own Right Time', sub-headed 'An Exploration of Clockwork Design'. It is, in its own field, a classic, being beautifully illustrated with diagrams of great precision. It is also written in such an entertaining and personal style that what, to many, could be an obscure and boring subject, jumps to life. The Curator of Horology at Greenwich described it as, 'A landmark in our horological literature.'

Philip Woodward was the recipient of the 1994 British Horological Institute Silver Medal. He has also had a building named after him. Following his days with the Defence Evaluation Research Agency the section in which Woodward worked was named 'The Woodward Building' and opened by the chief executive of DERA, Sir John Chisholm.

Guy Julier (M 1974-1979) is the son of the long-serving (but now retired) Blundell's Art Master, Robert Julier. His special interest in life, and the subject on which he has written a host of articles and had four books published, is Design. Having completed five years at Blundell's, Guy Julier went on to Manchester University where he got a BA, having read History of Art. He then went to the Royal College of Art and gained a MA in History of Design. Next he continued to pursue his interest in Spain, where he lived in Barcelona. When he returned to the UK he became Professor of Design and Critical Studies at Leeds Metropolitan University.

His four books, published from 1991 onwards, are 'New Spanish Design', a hardback from Thames and Hudson, also published in Spain, Germany, and the United States; 'Mariscal Design', which was written in Spanish; 'The Encyclopaedia of 20th Century Design', which has been reprinted several times; and 'The Culture of Design', which has a big, specialised, academic following.

IN CONCLUSION

I hope these notes on Blundellian writers over the past 400 years have held your interest and thrown some light on the achievements of the school. It is up to you to judge how Blundellian writers stand by the Rab Butler criteria. Your verdicts will be interesting, but what will be even more interesting is how Blundell's will perform in the future. Now the school has been co-educational for over twenty years, perhaps we will soon see female writers emerging; and it remains to be seen if our present writers (men like Lloyd-Jones, Hollands, Swain, Fox, Ondaatje, and Rice) can consolidate their reputations and stand the test of time, as have Blackmore, Joad, Sir John Squire, and Michael Shanks, to name just a few.